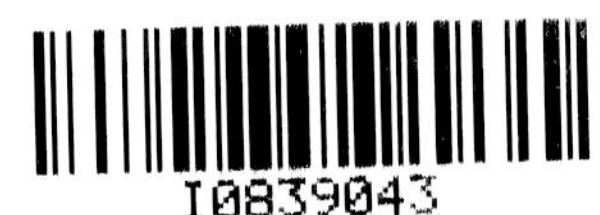

Coloring book for adults and kids amazing panda image for design

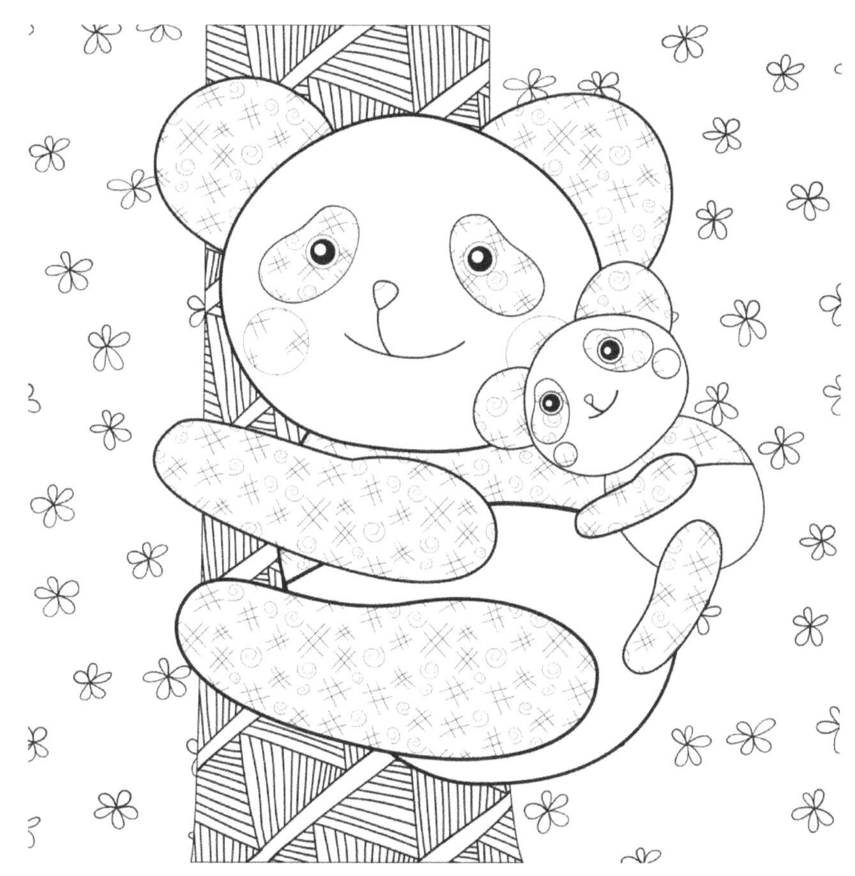

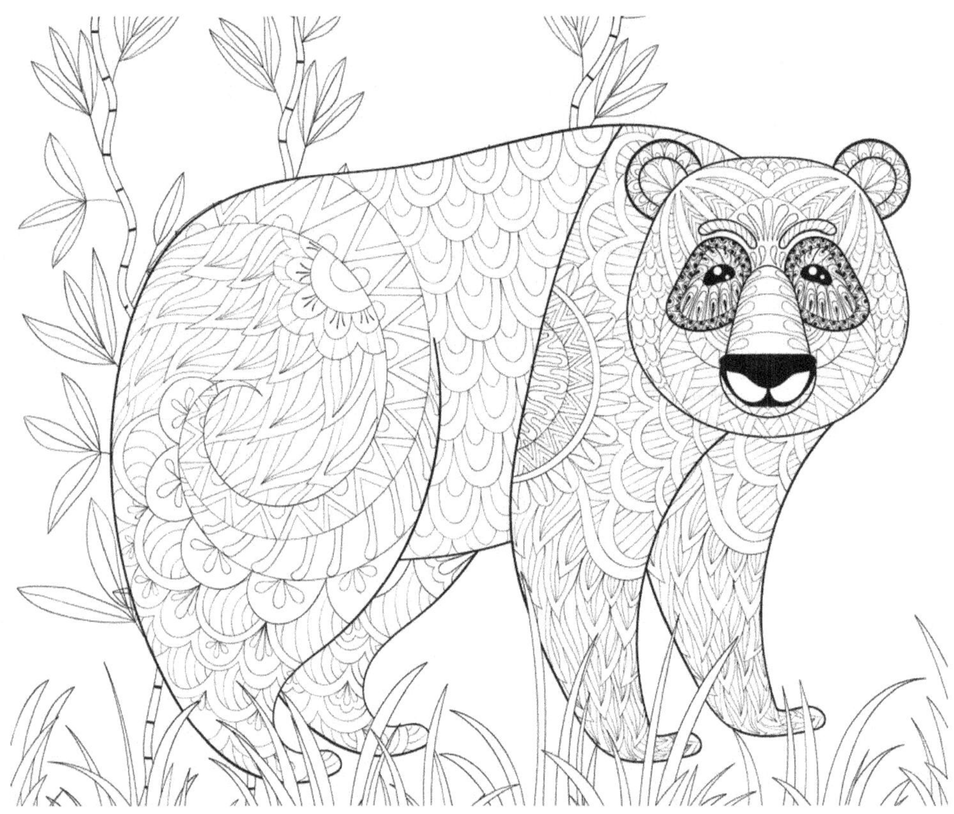

This coloring book is belongs to

____

____

____

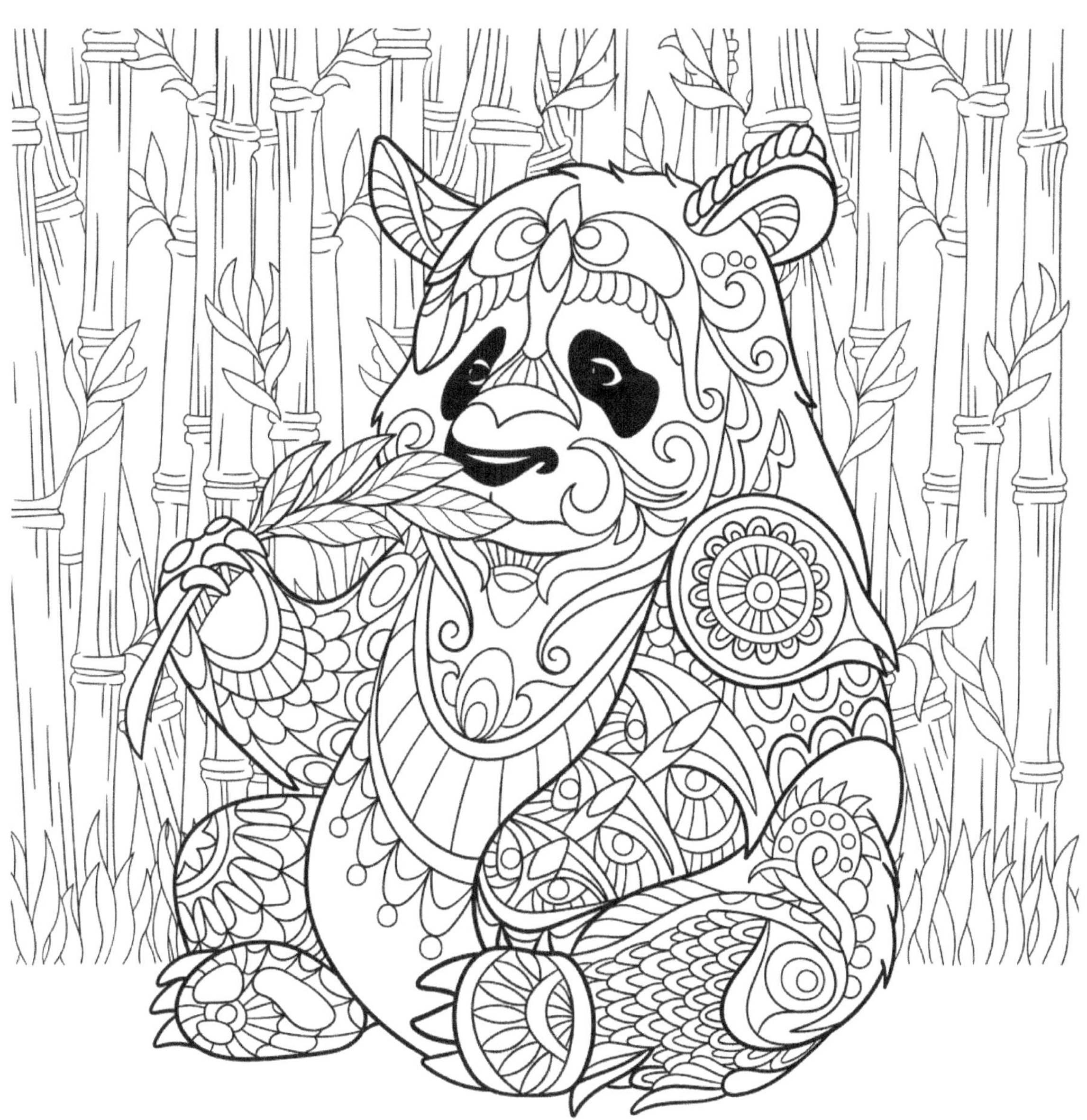

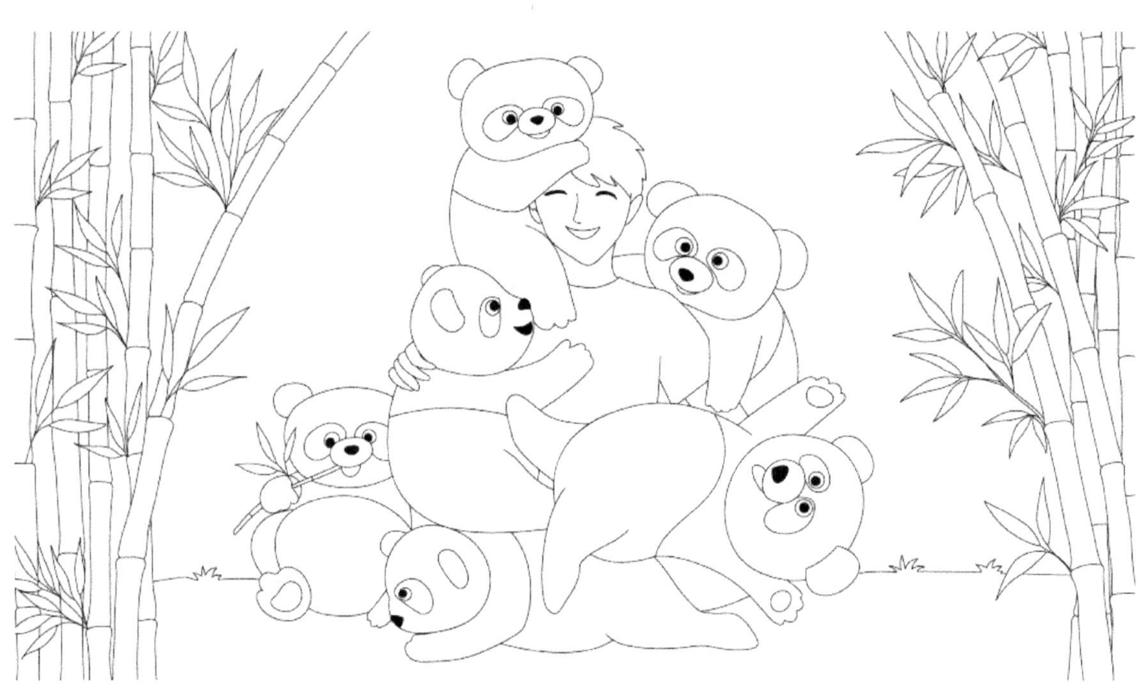

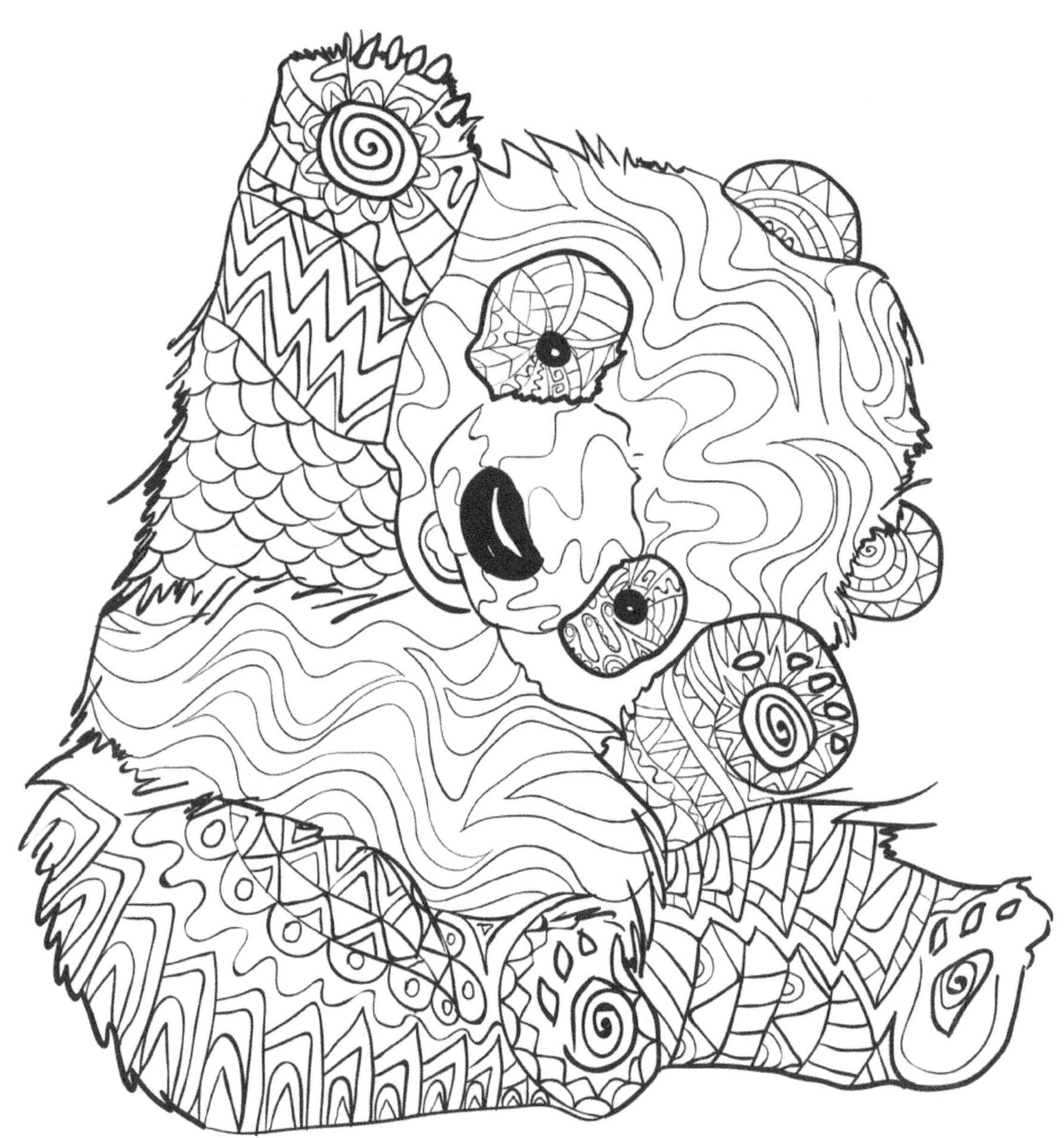

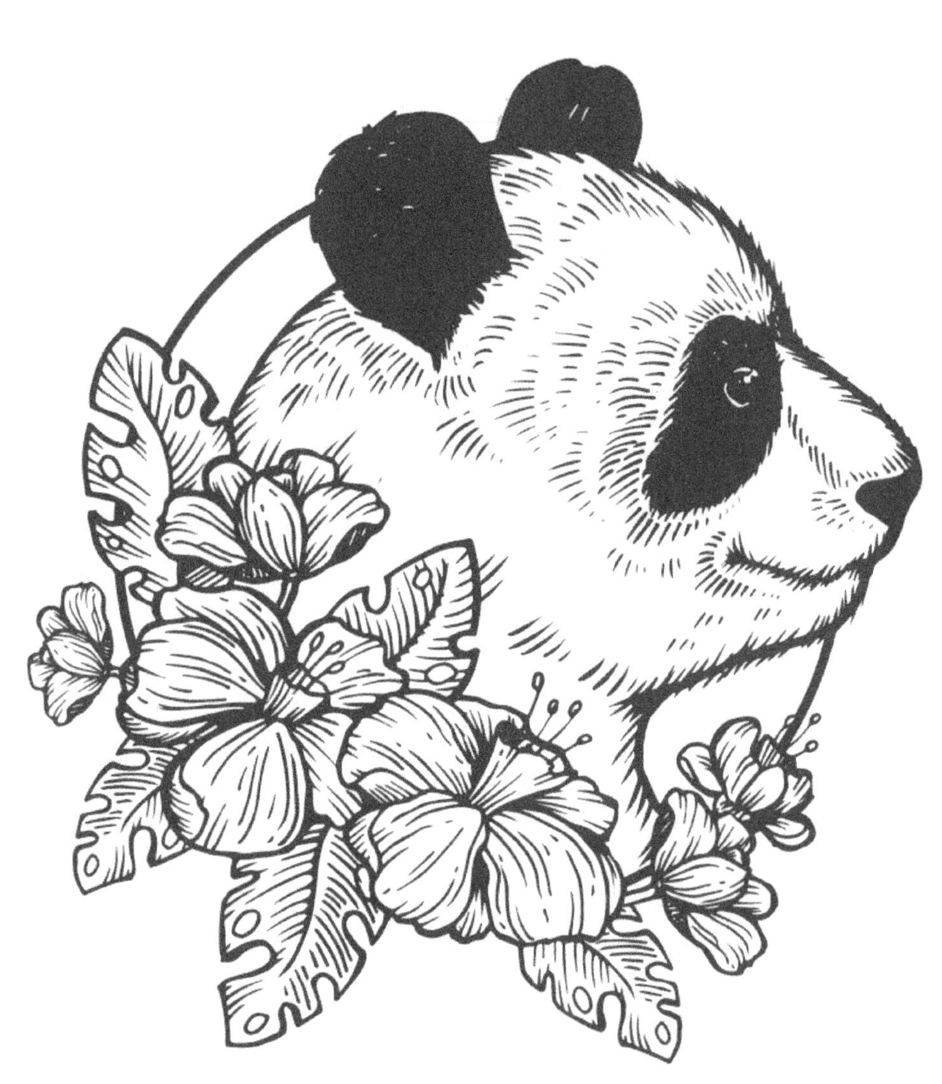

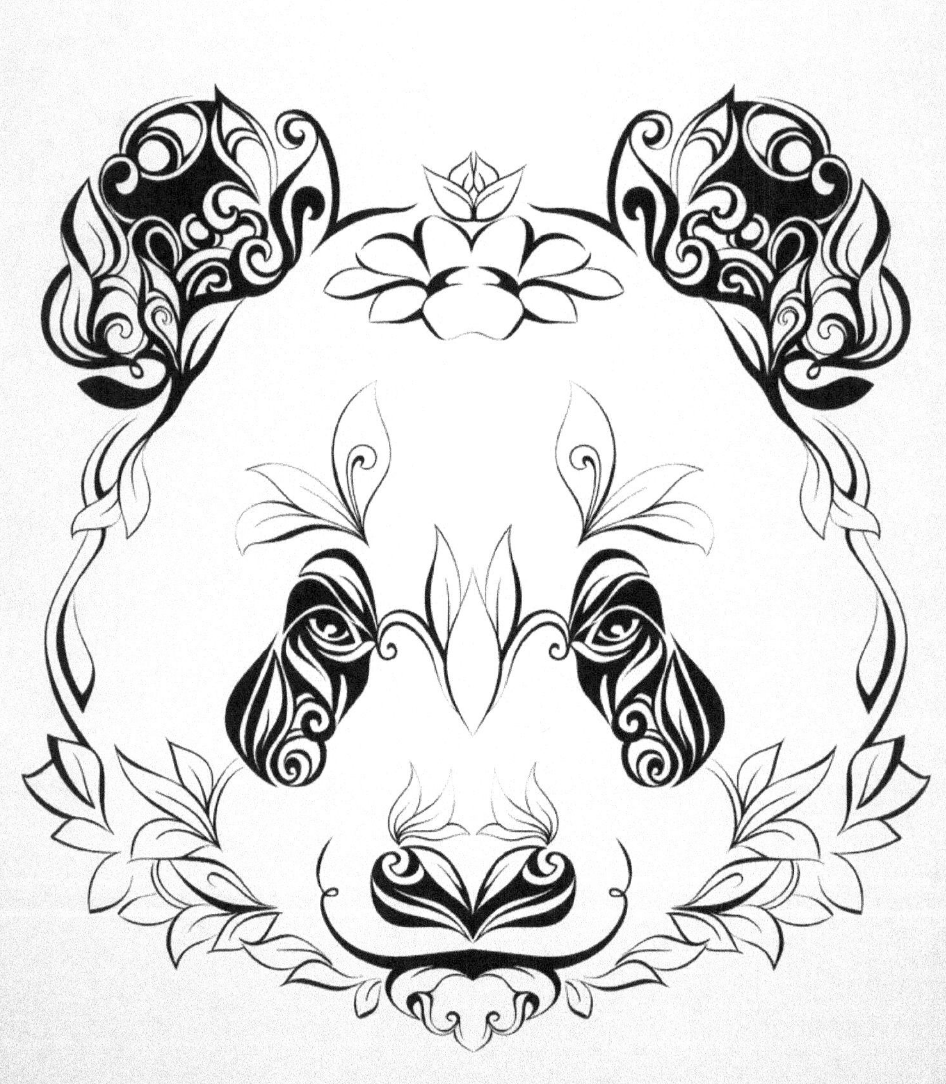

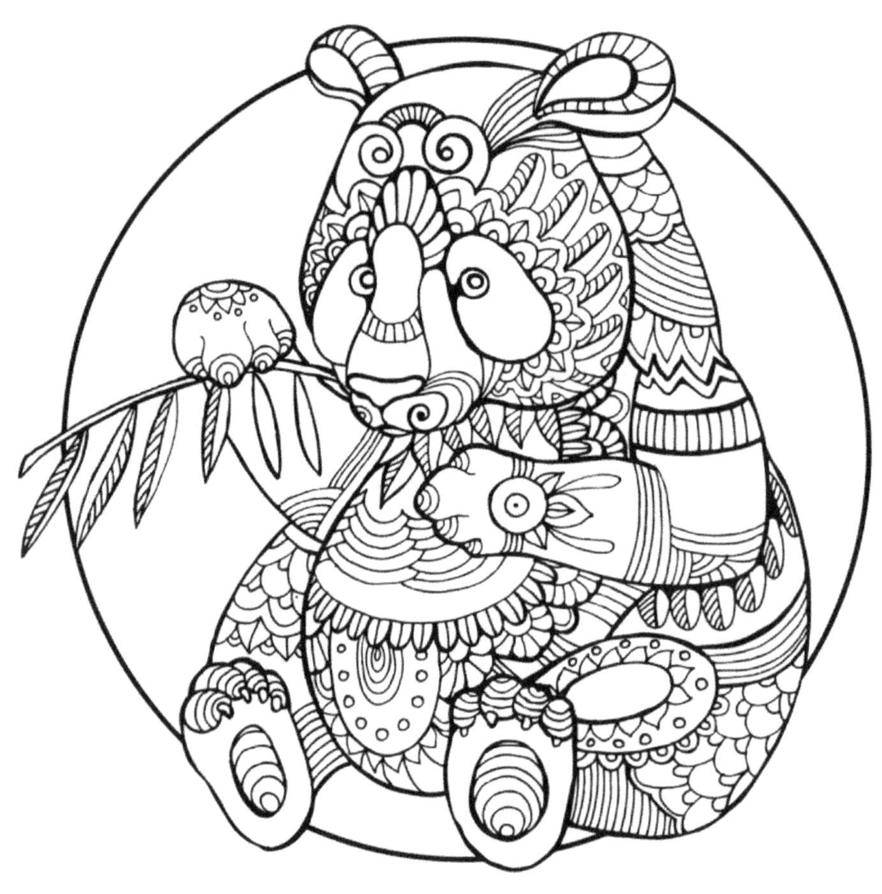

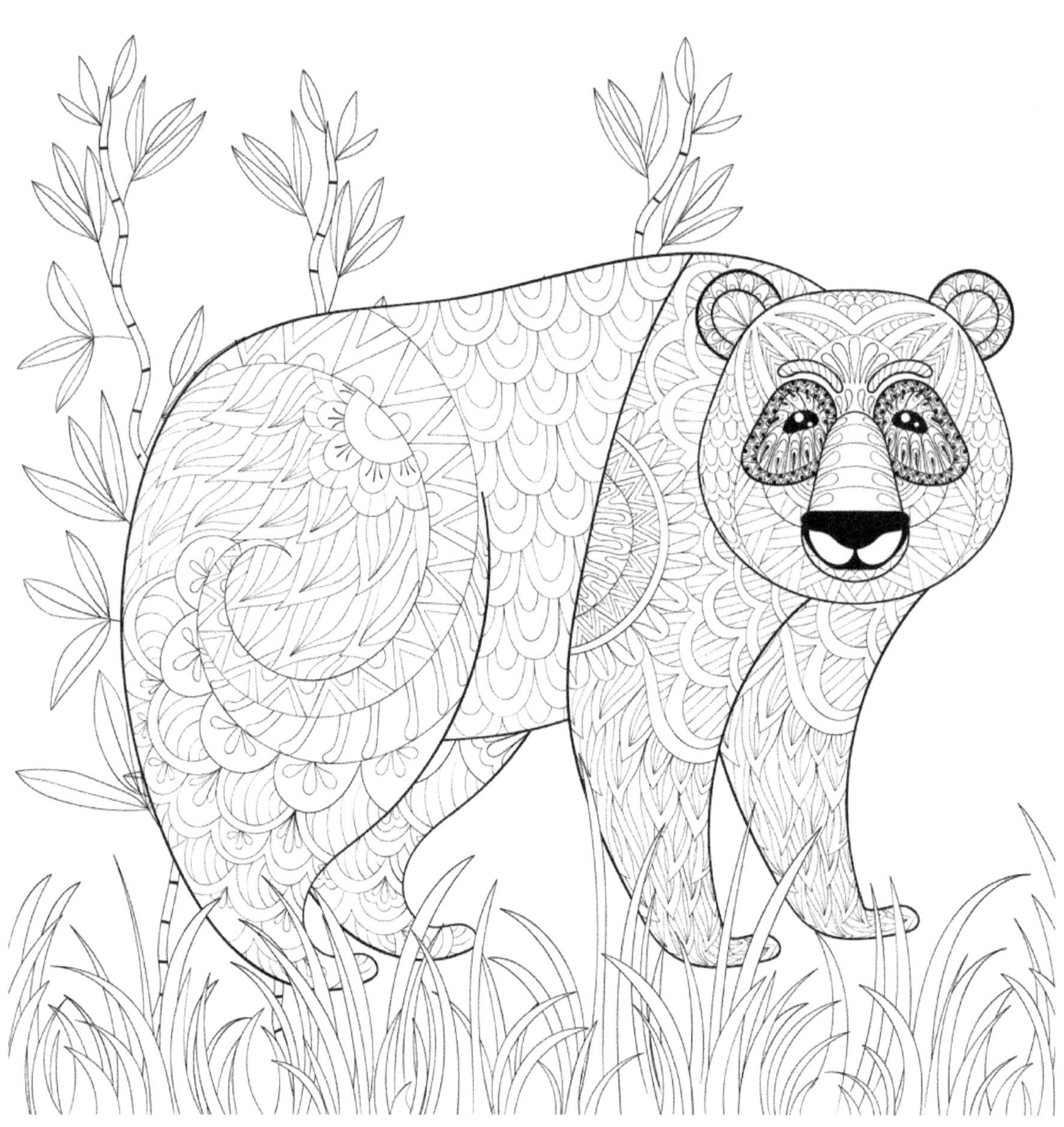

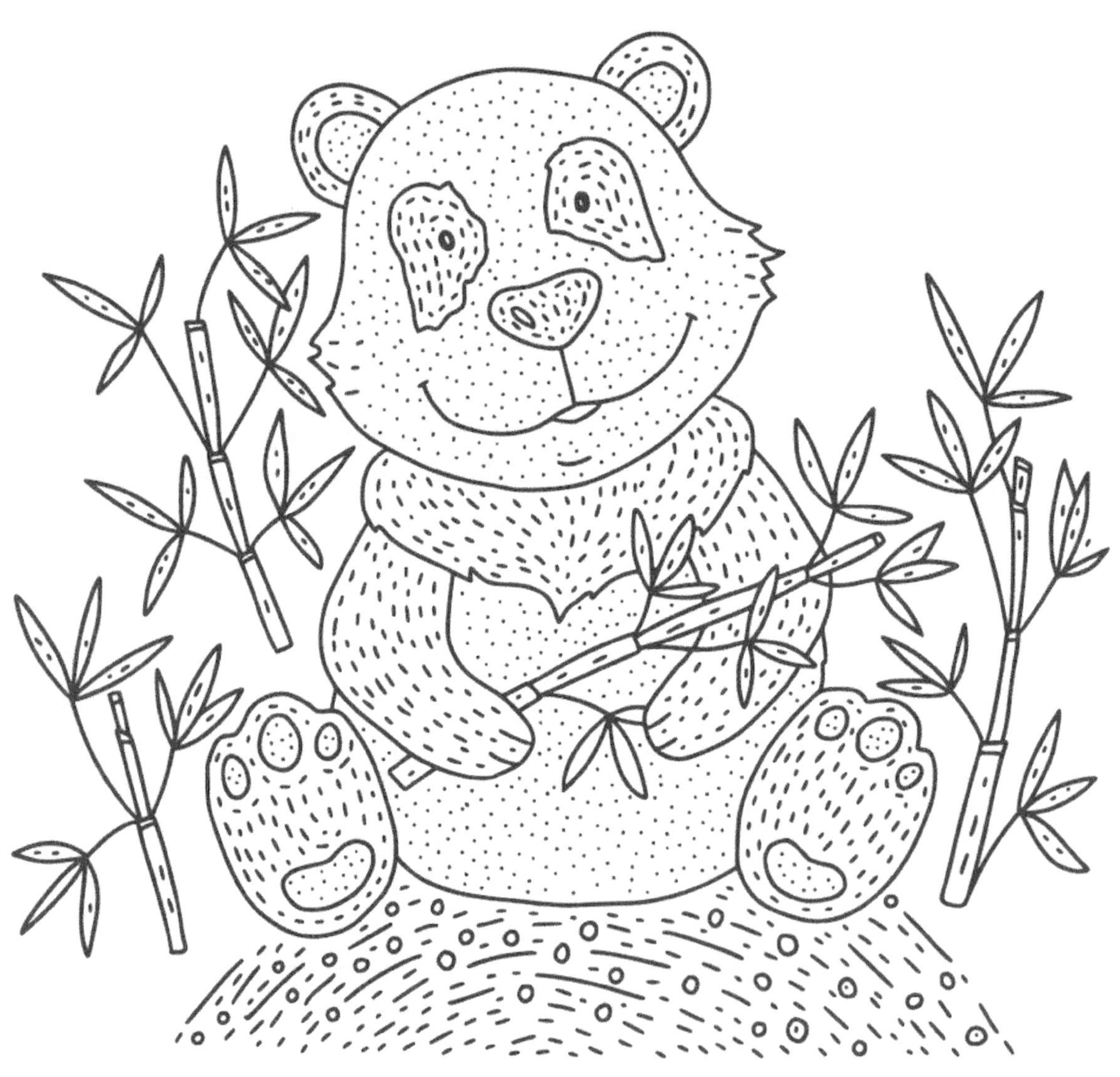

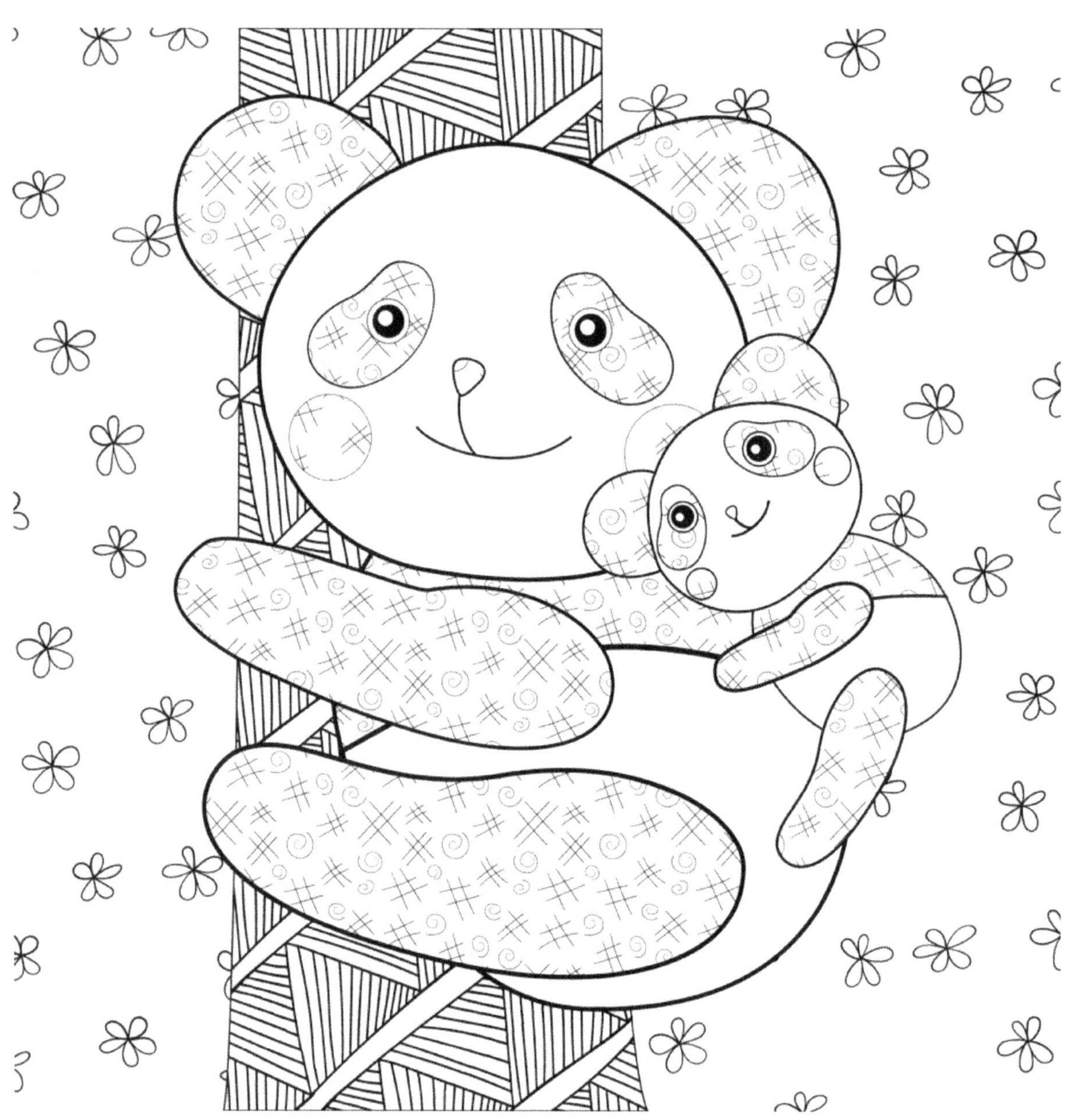

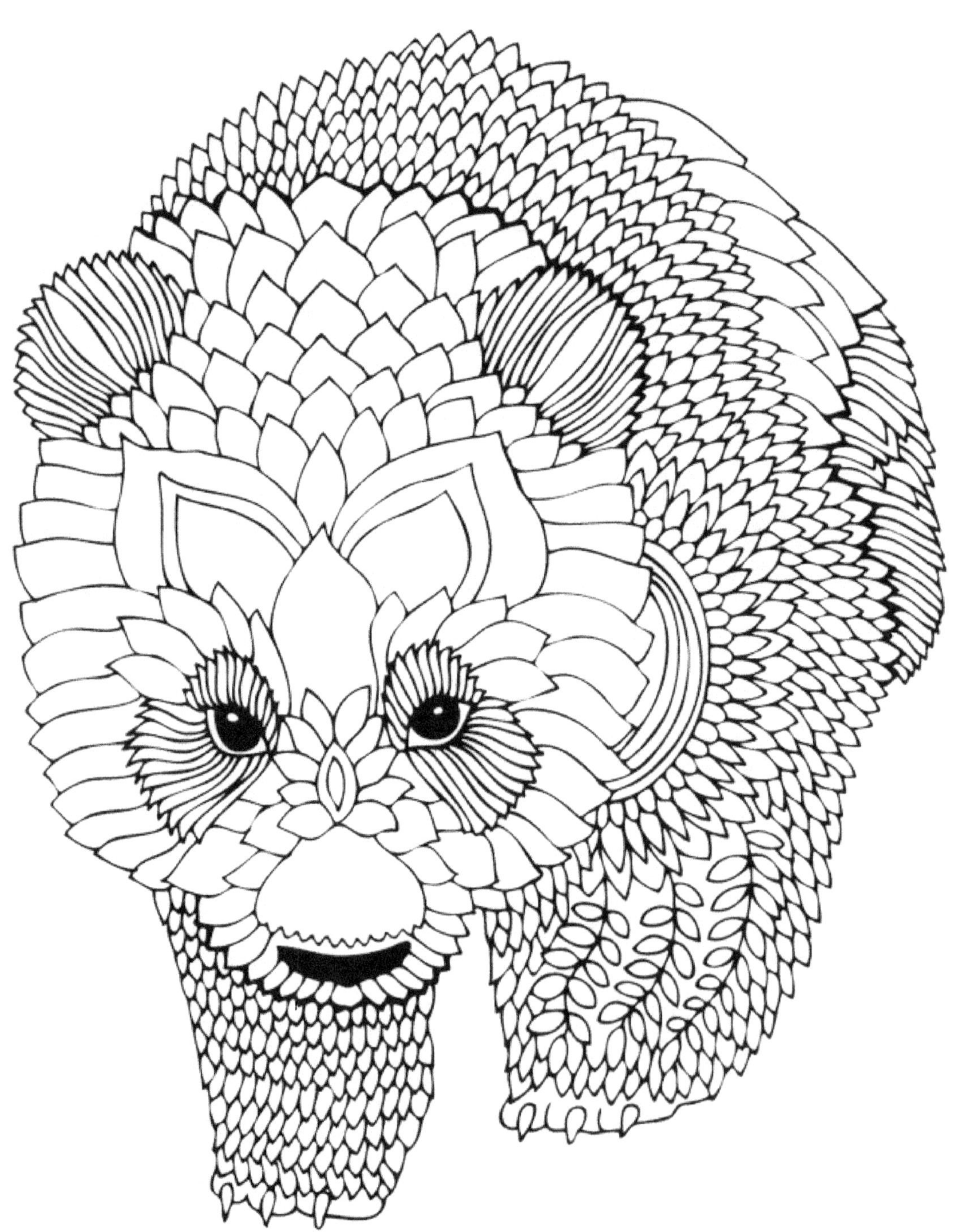

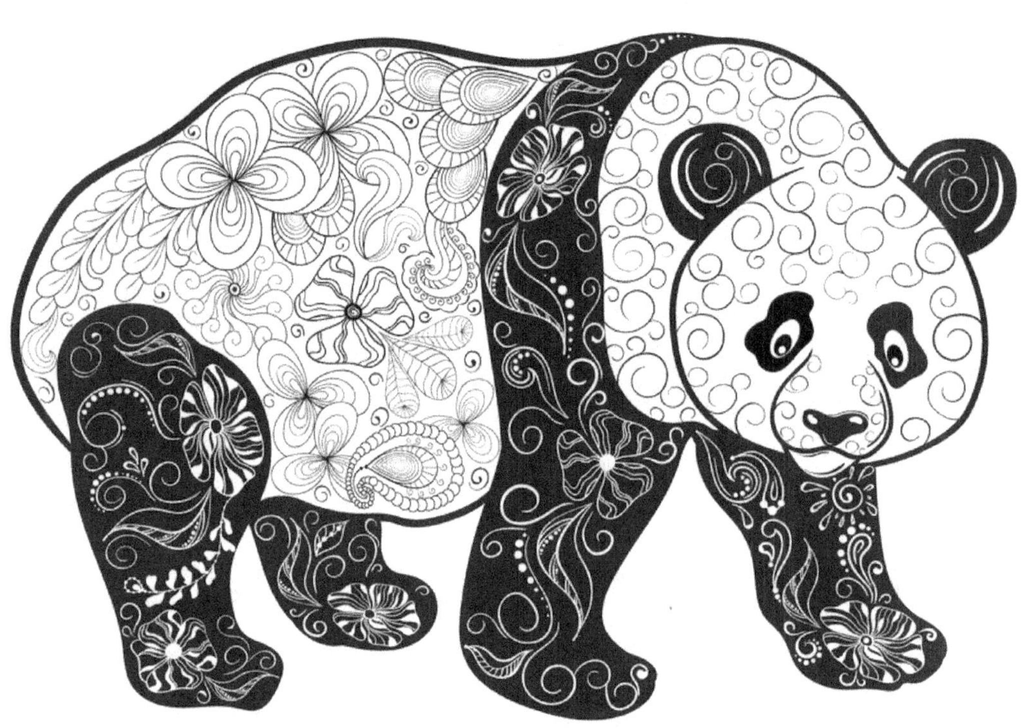

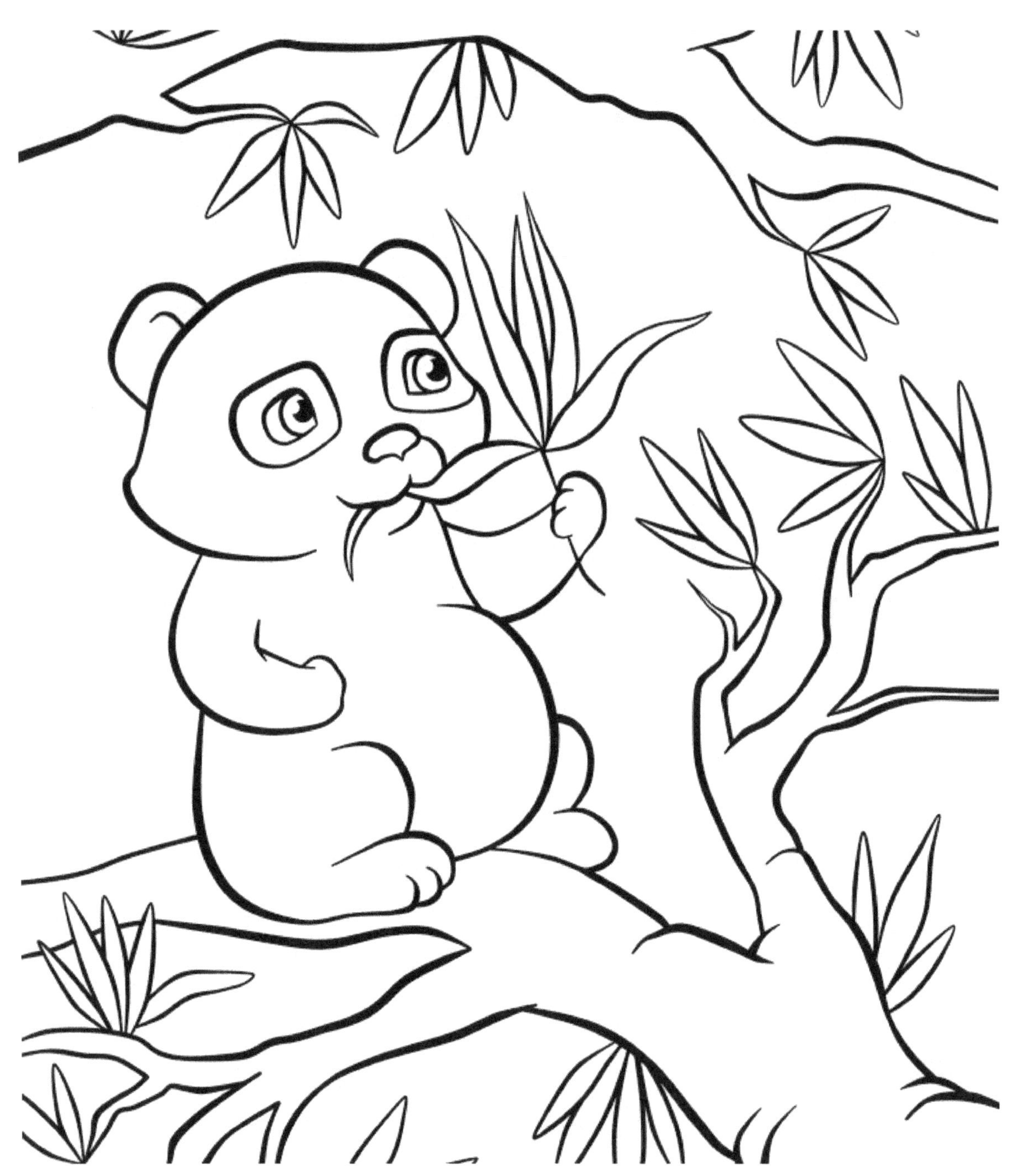

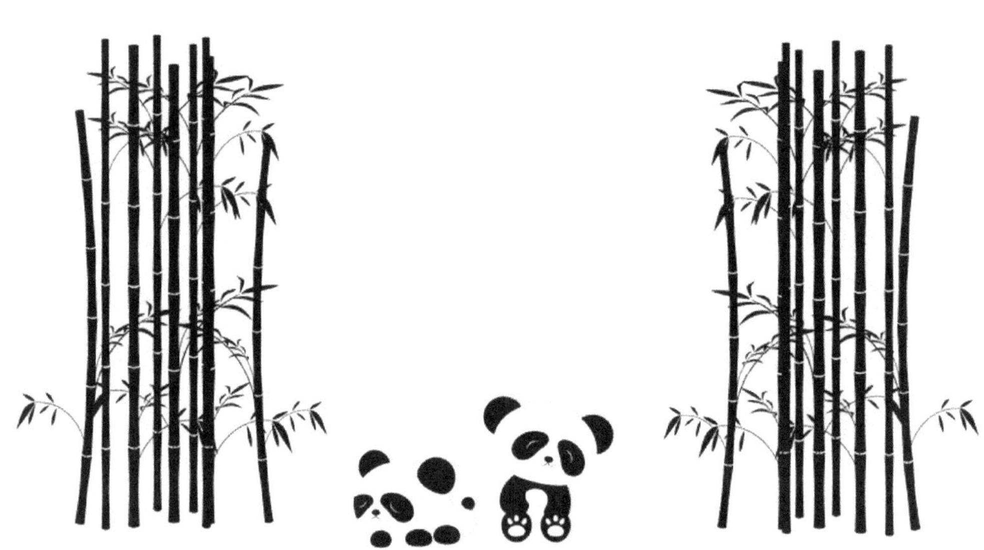

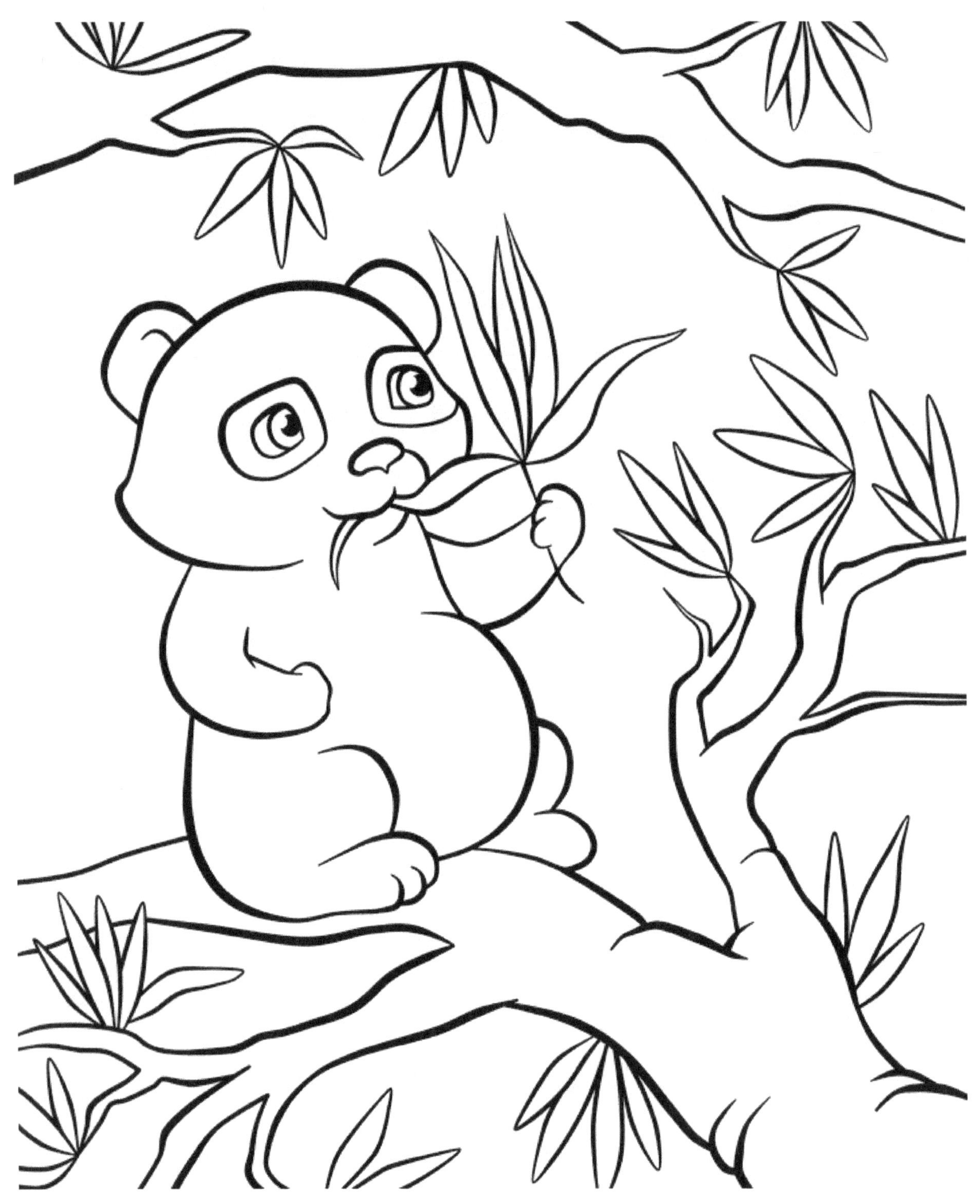

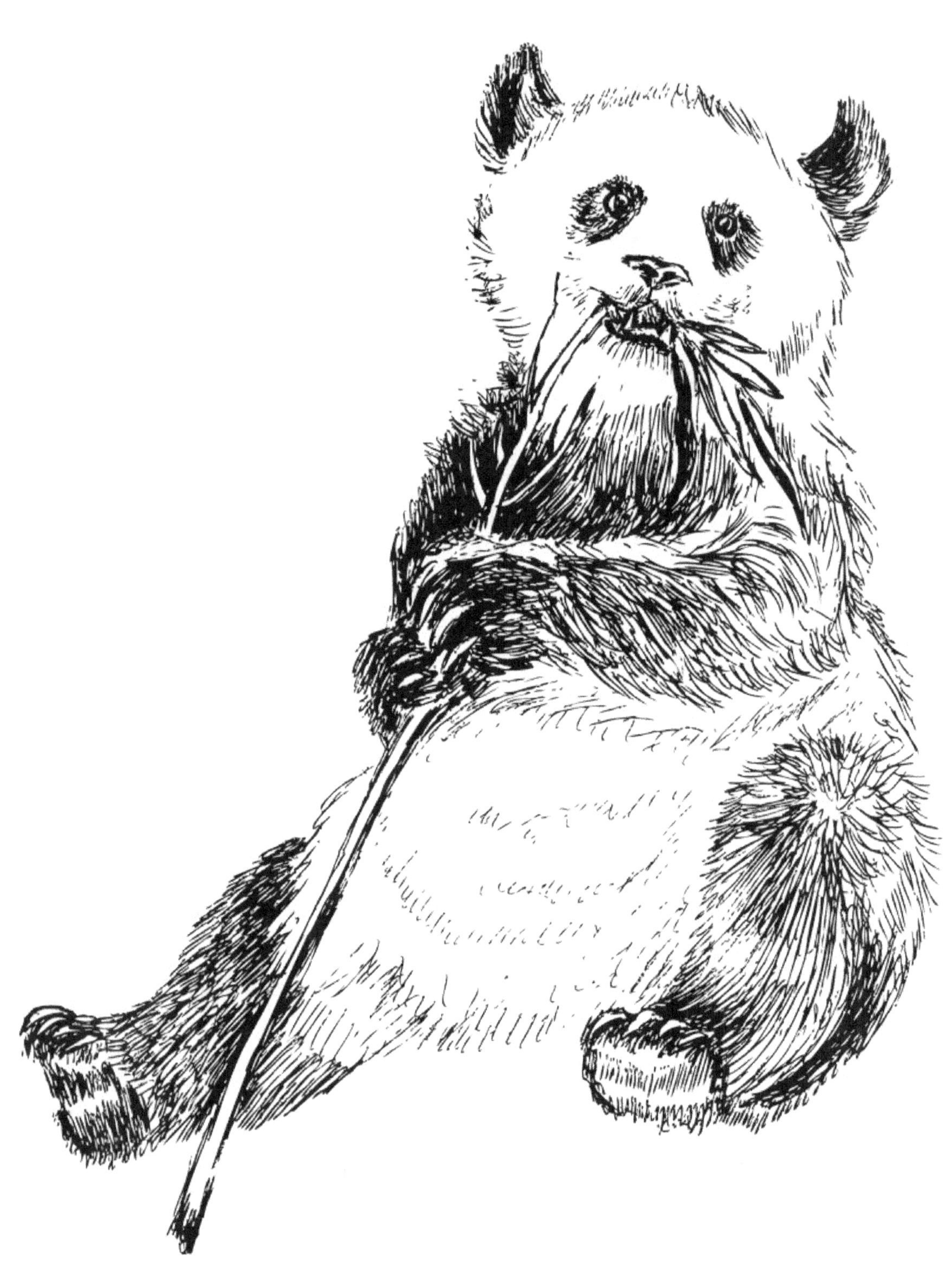

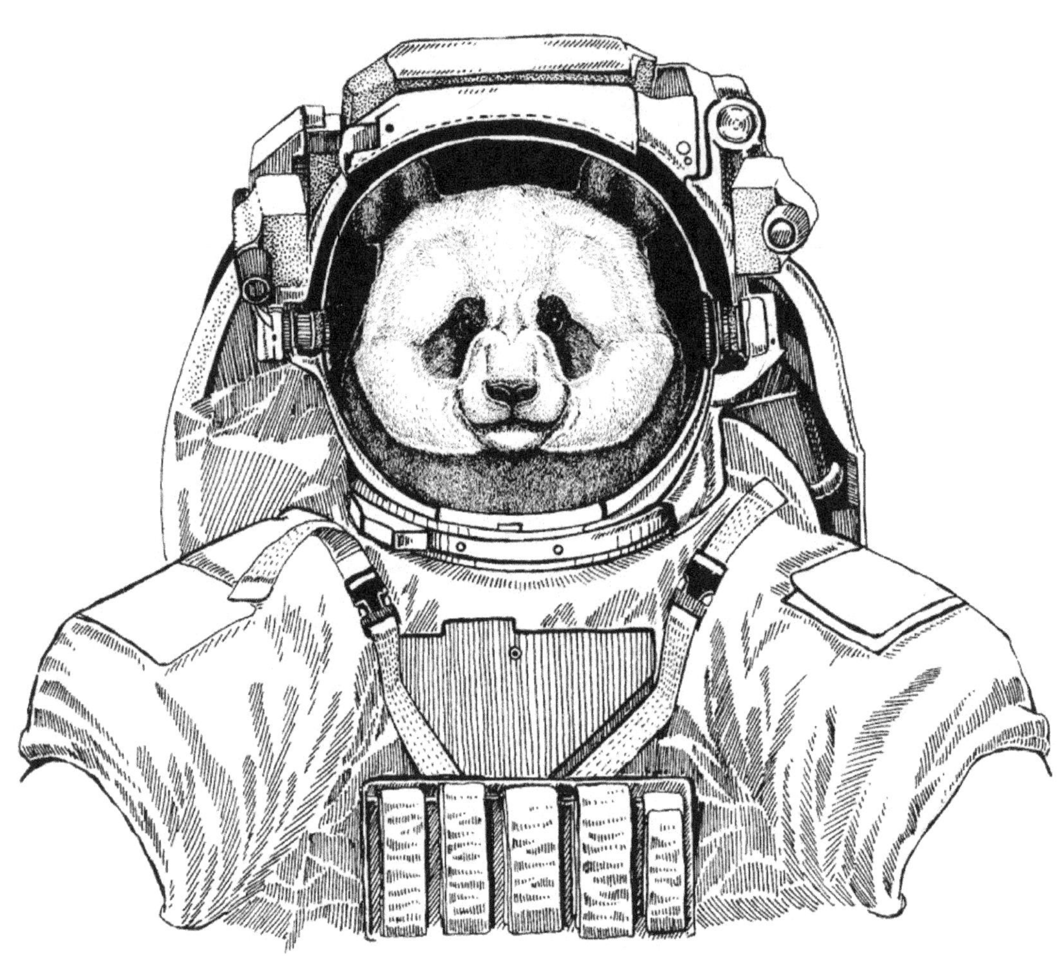

I NEED MORE SPACE

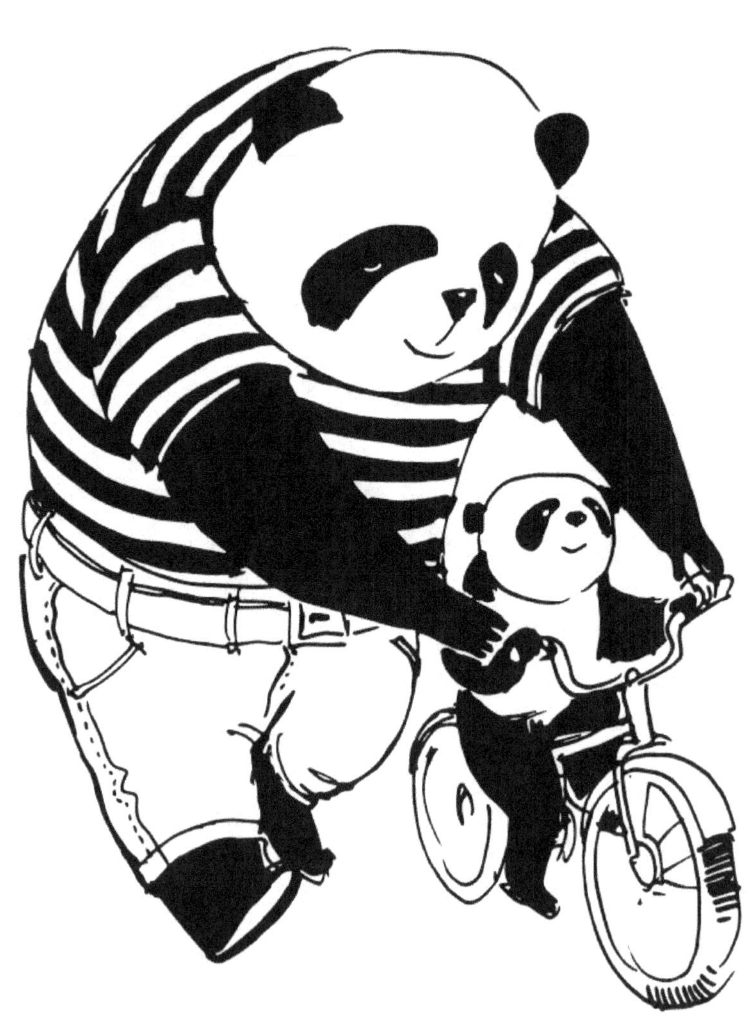

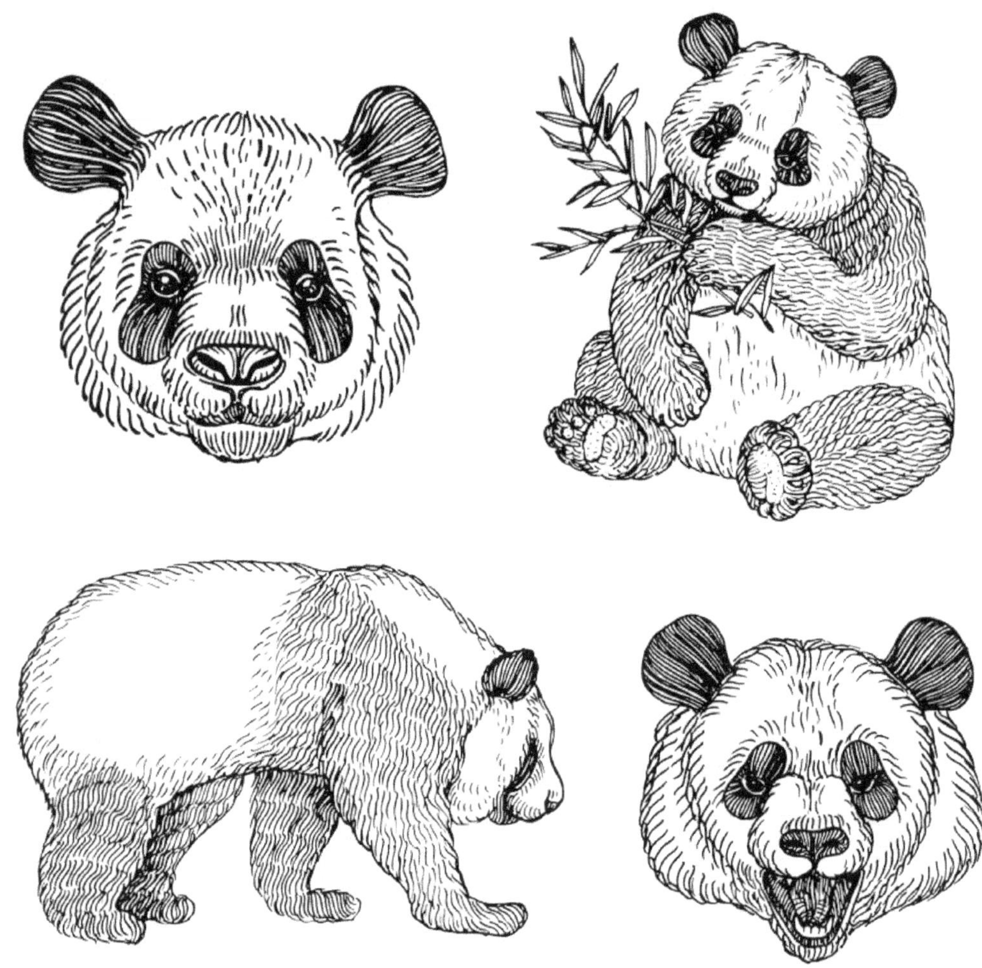

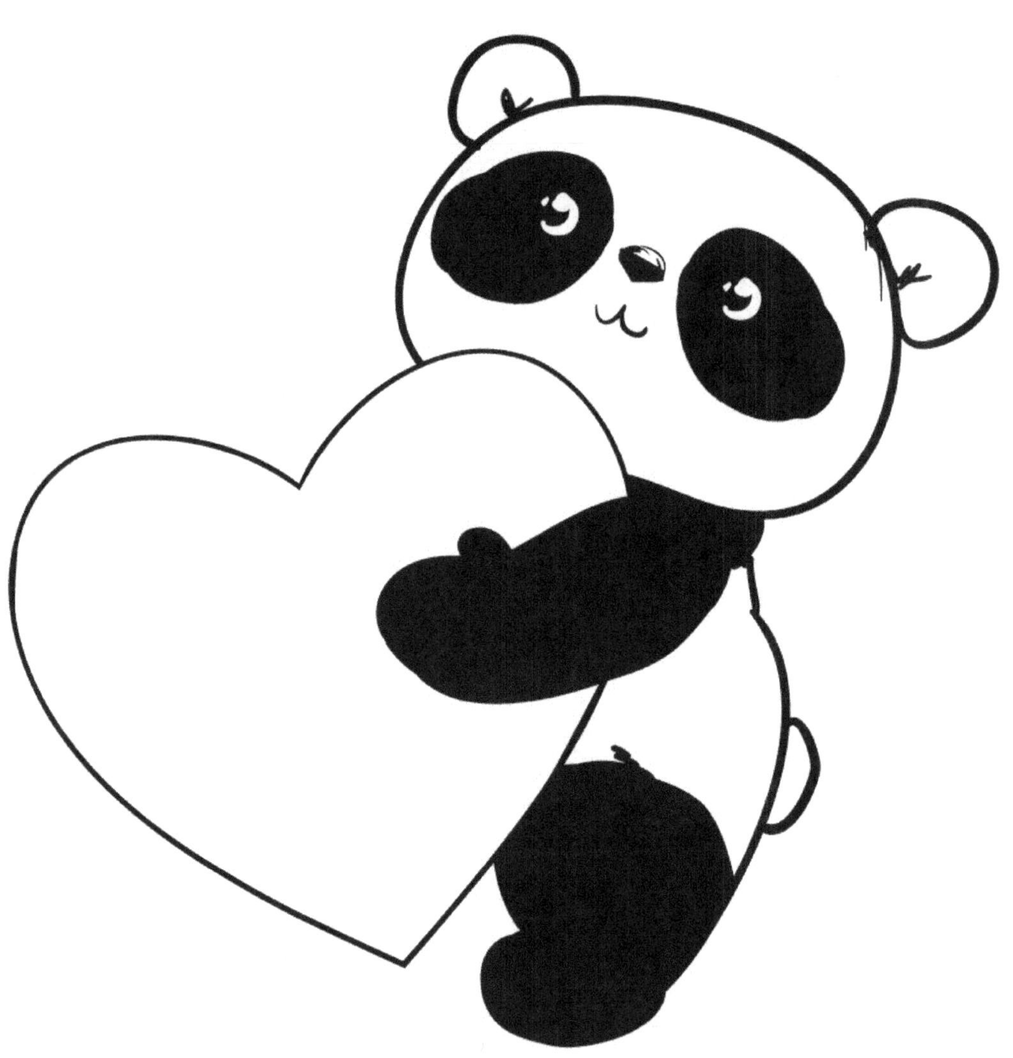

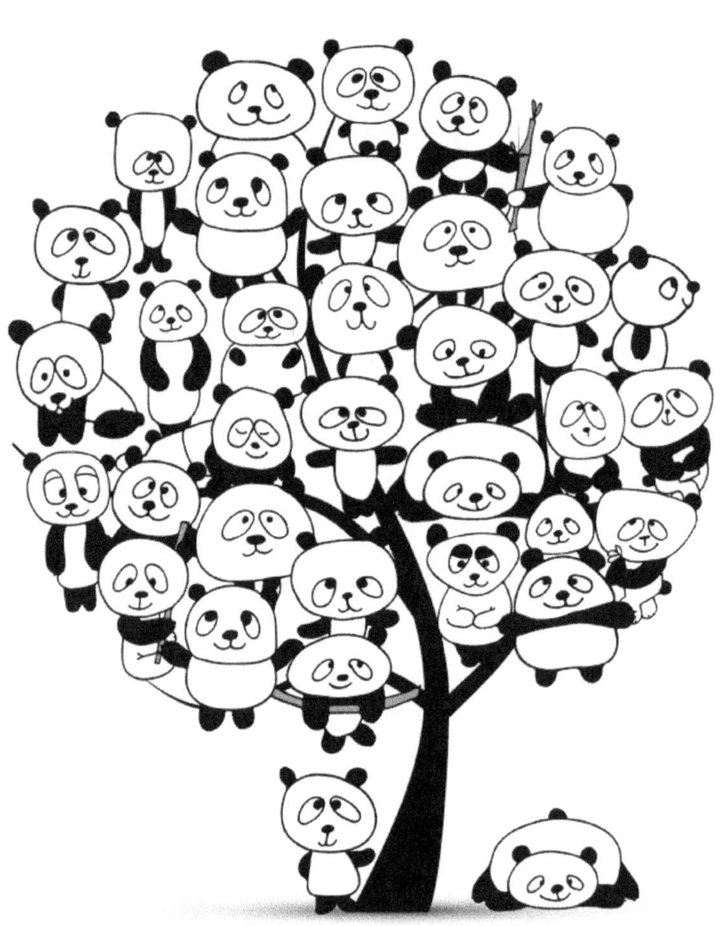

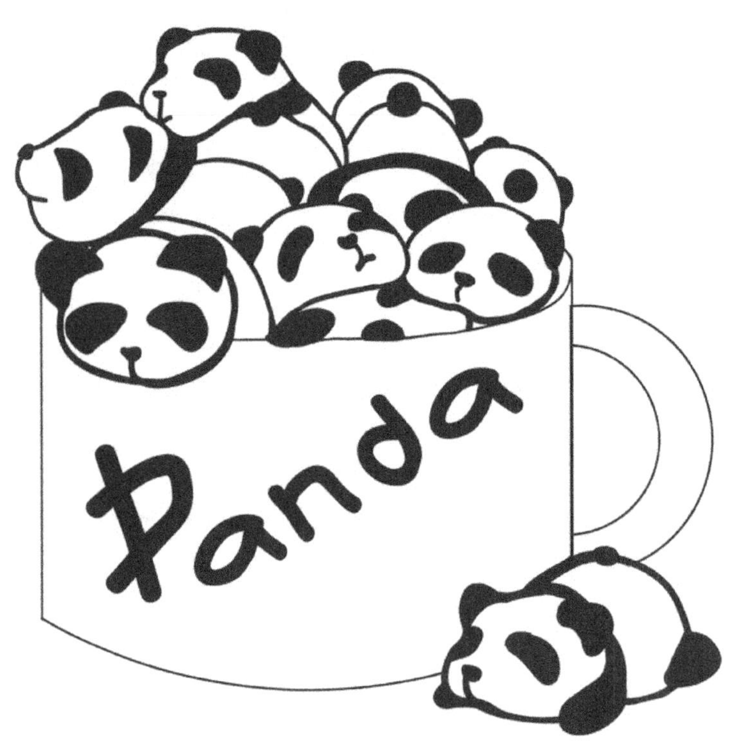
Panda

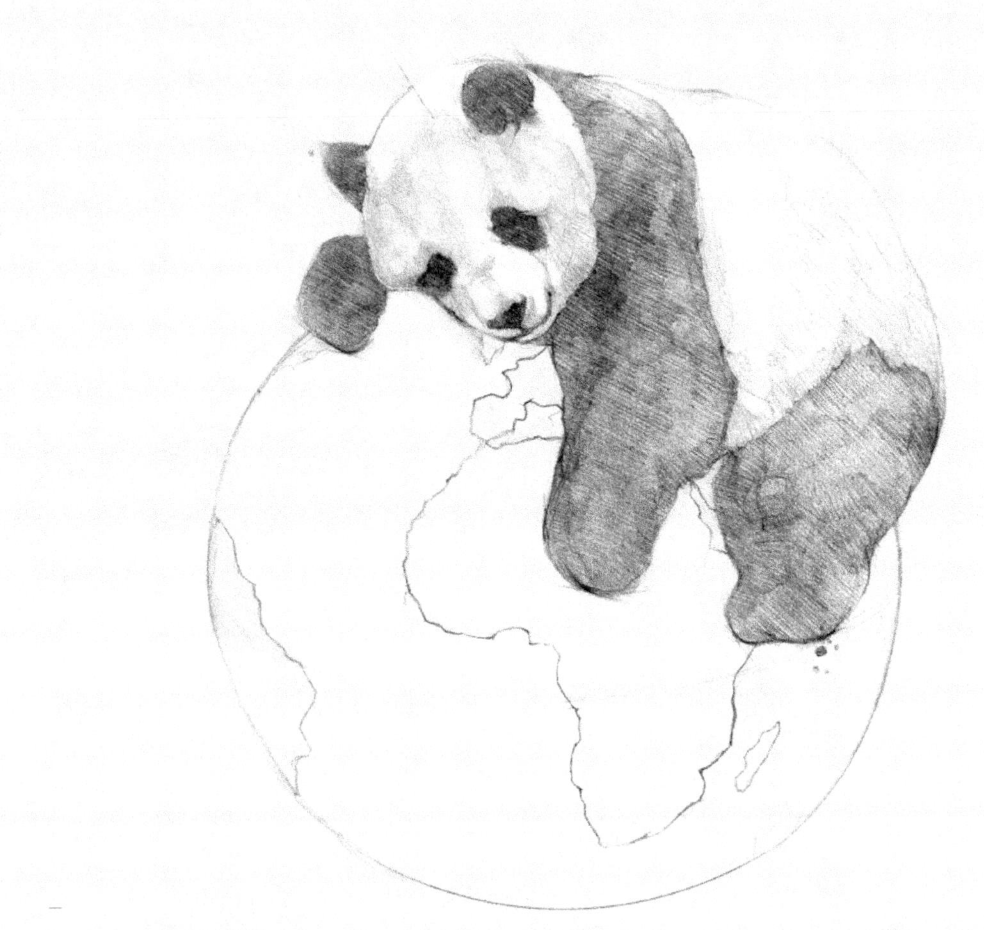

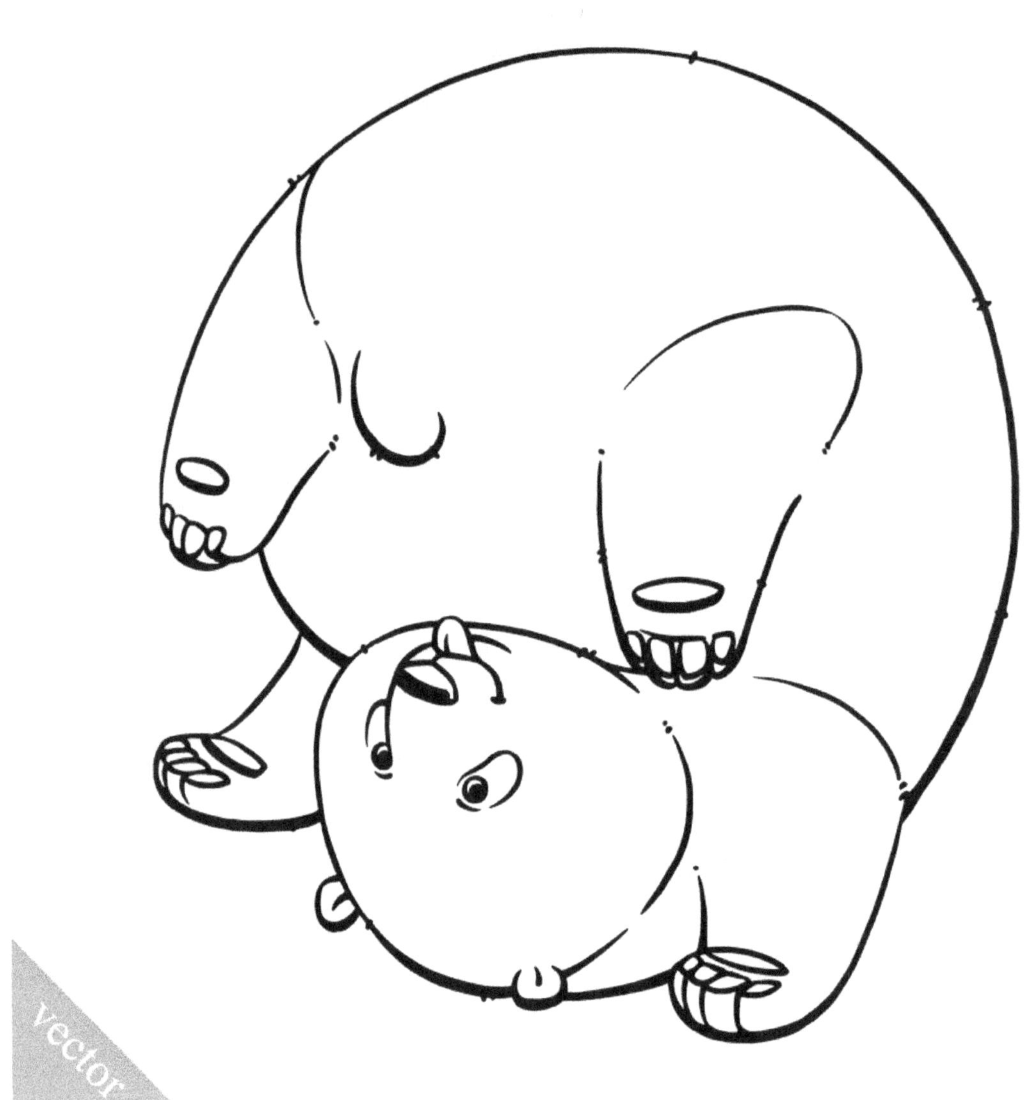

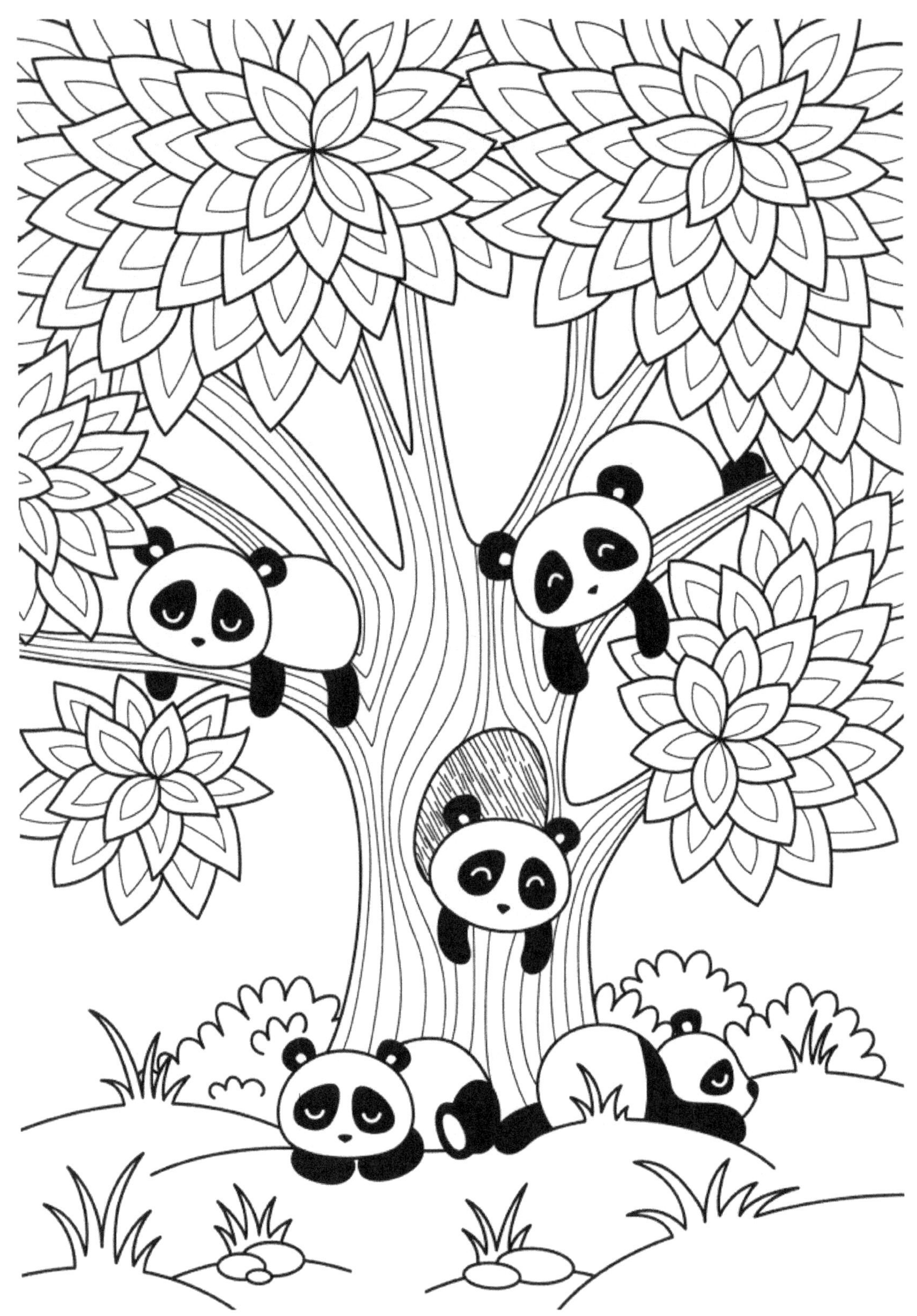

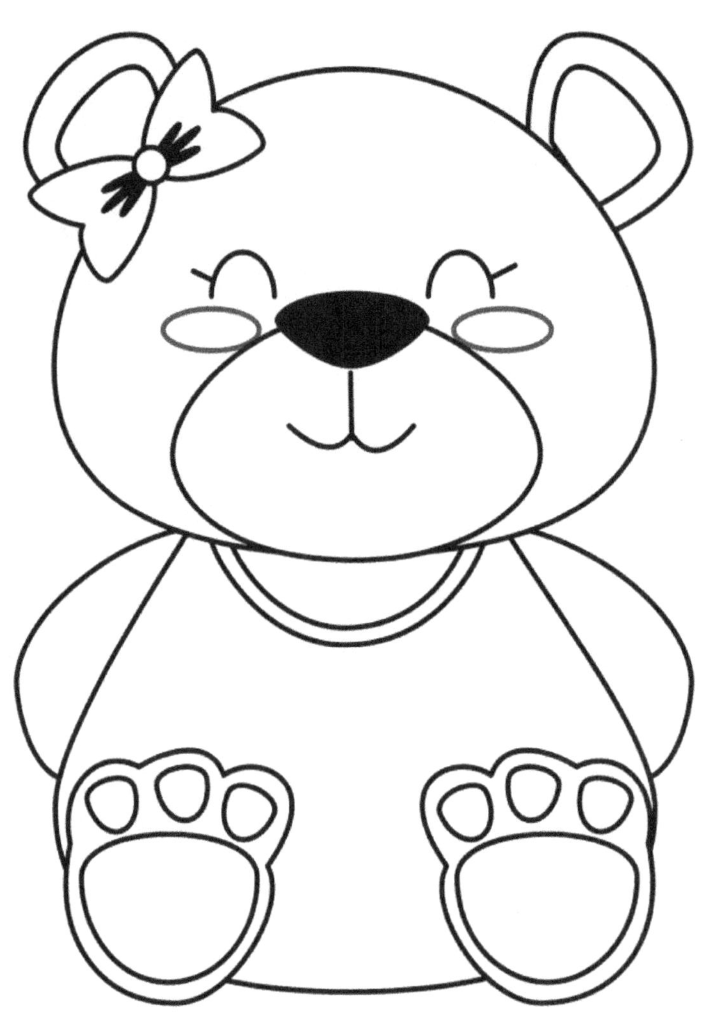

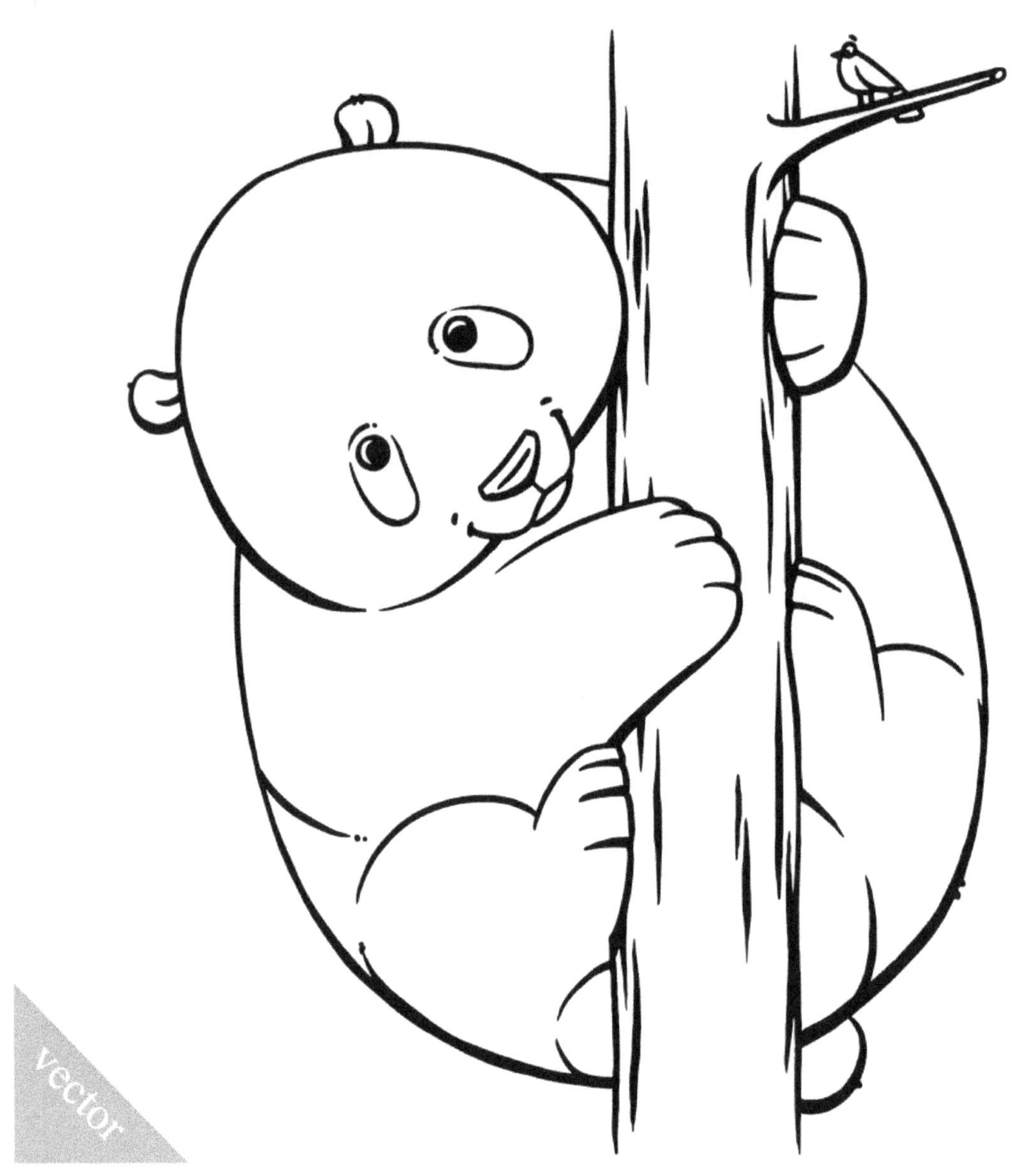

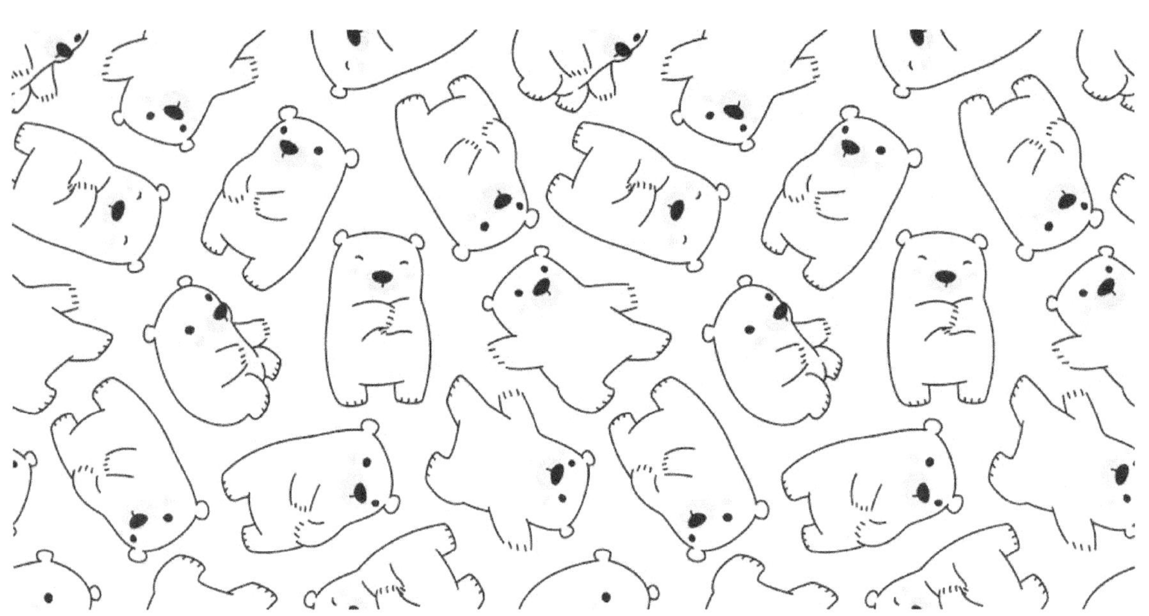

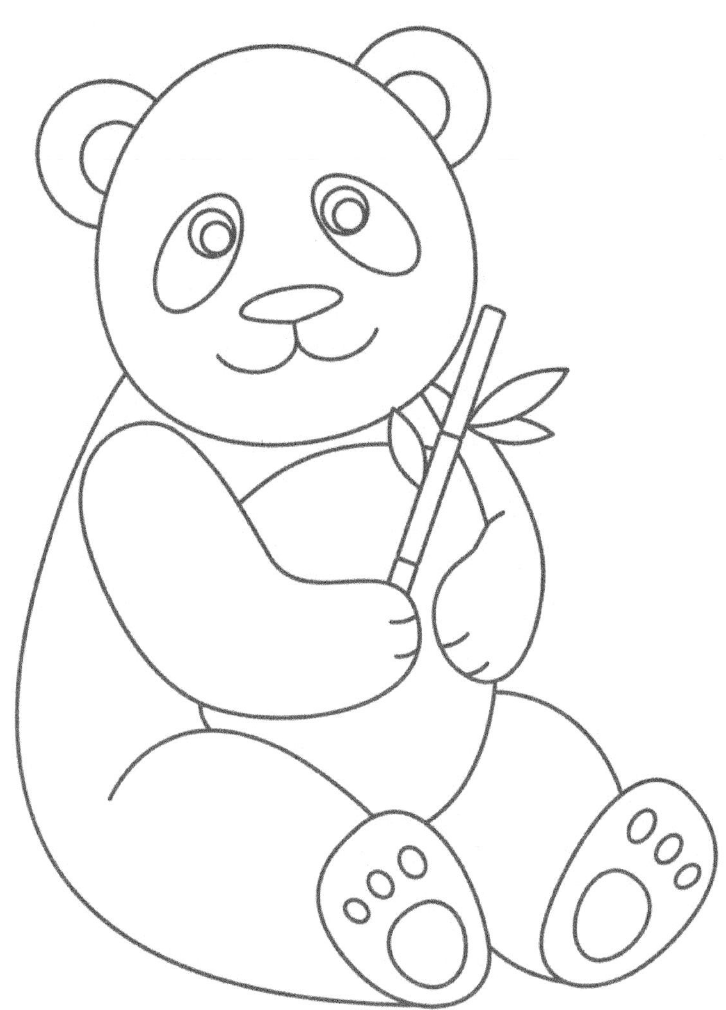

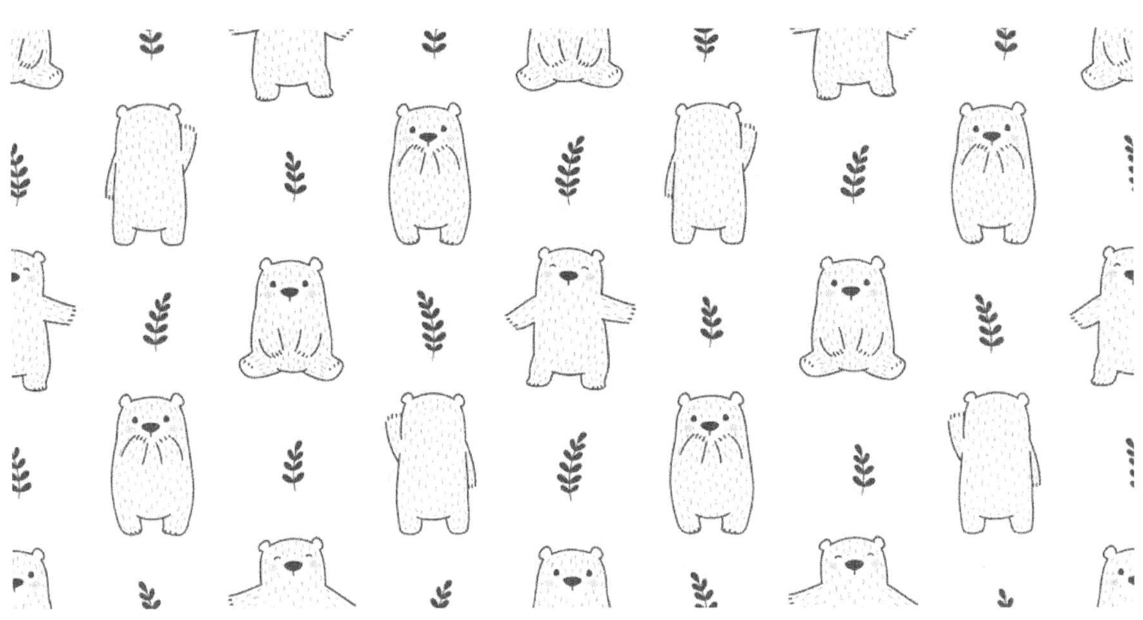

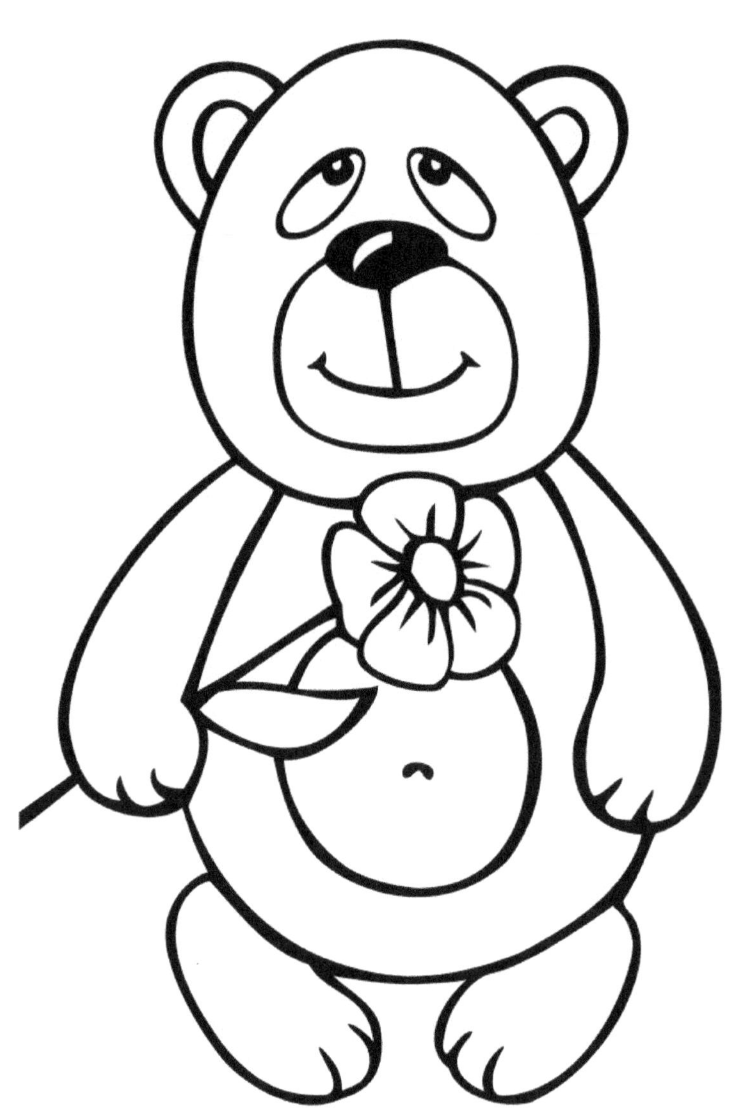

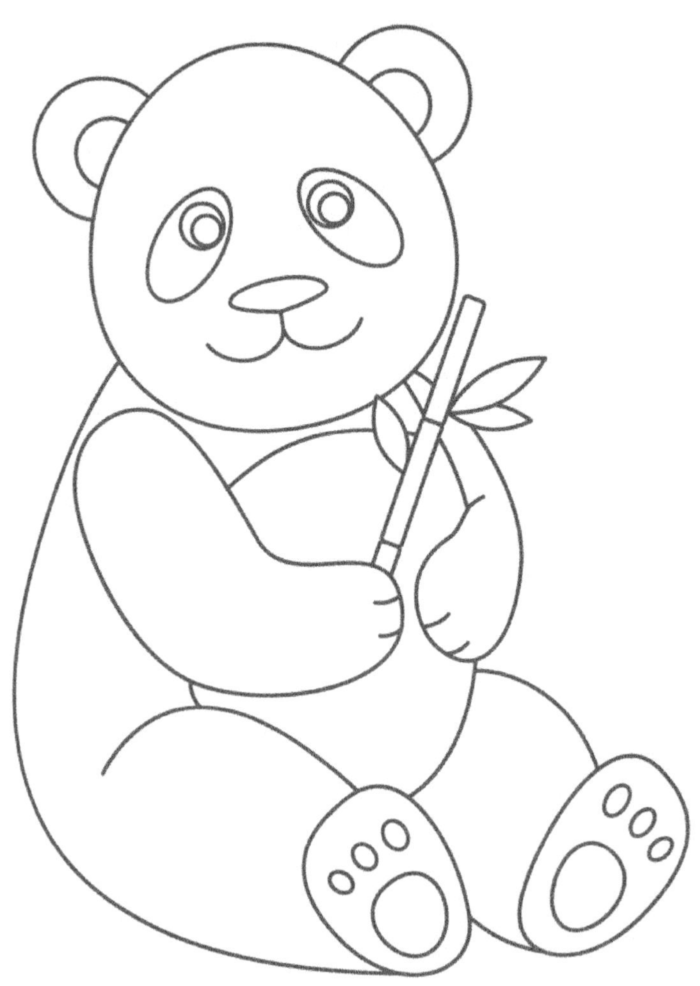

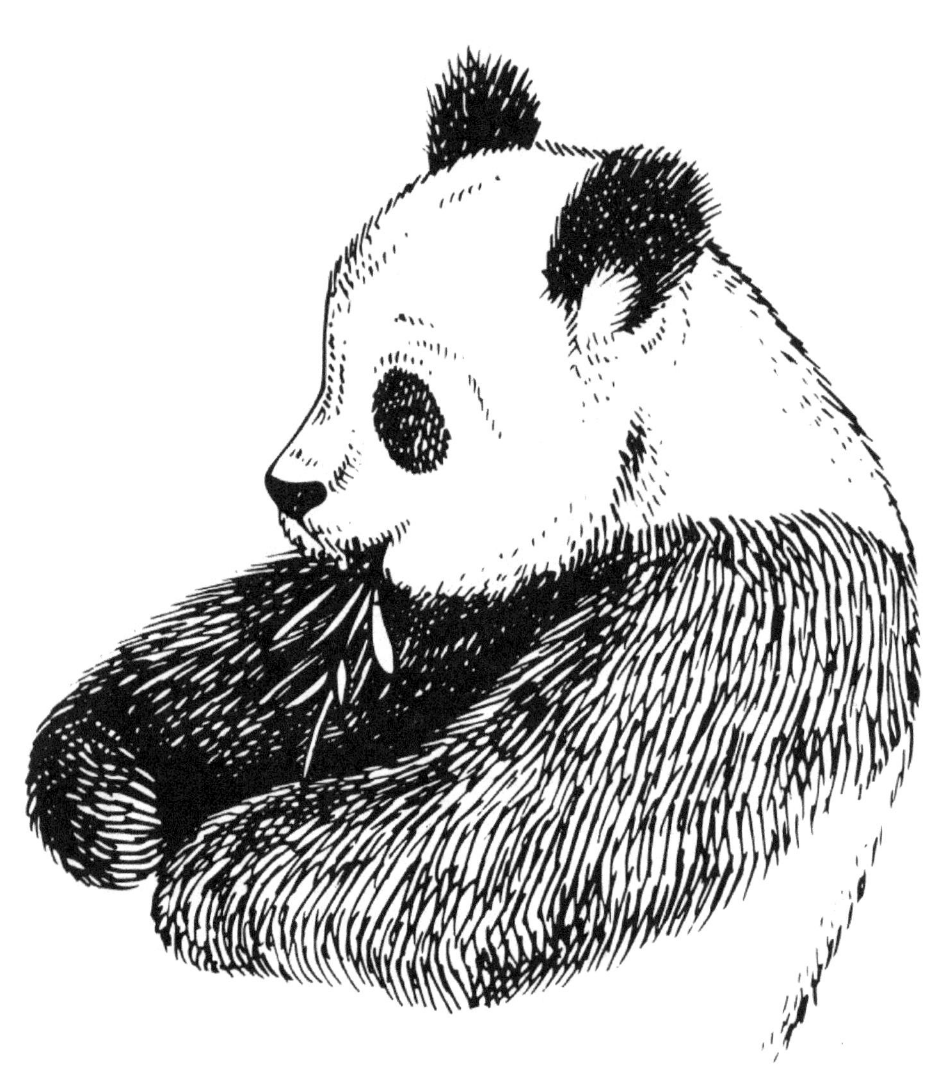

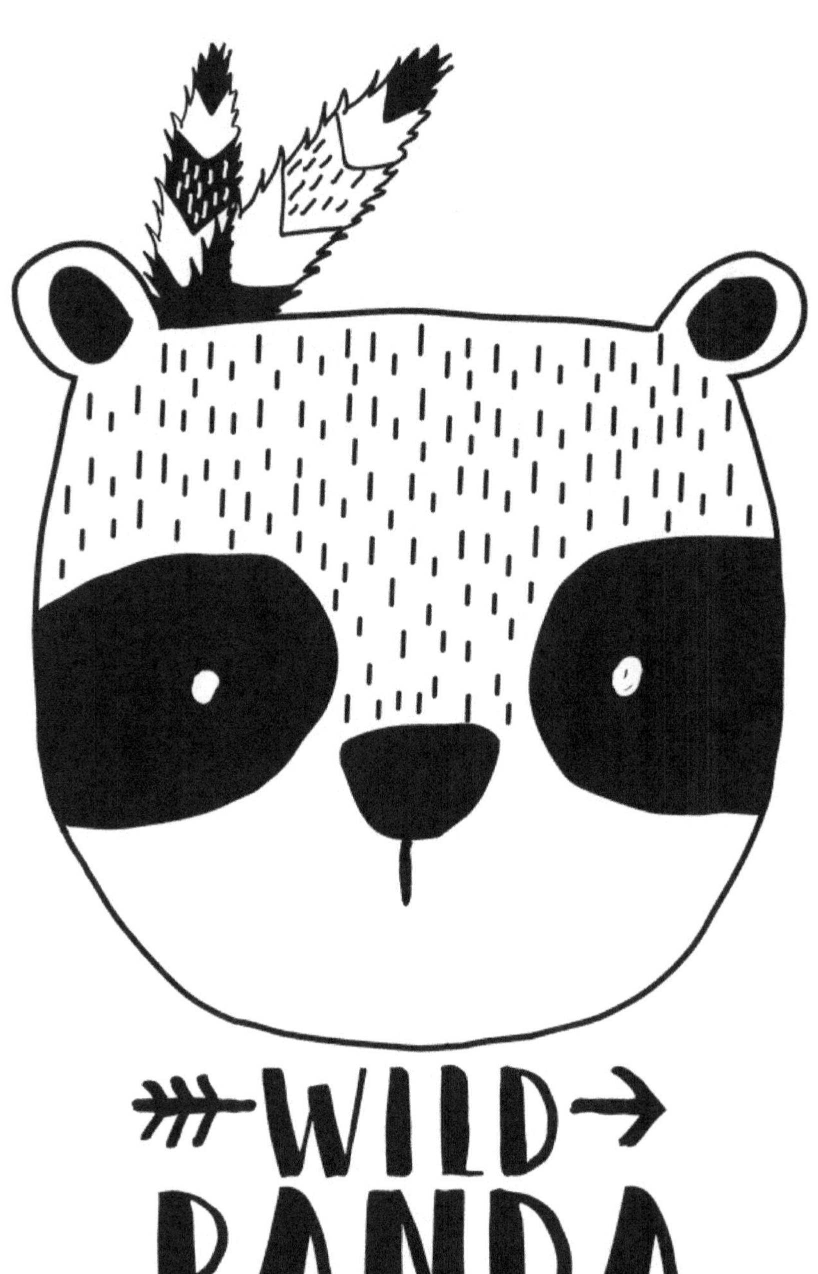

WILD
PANDA

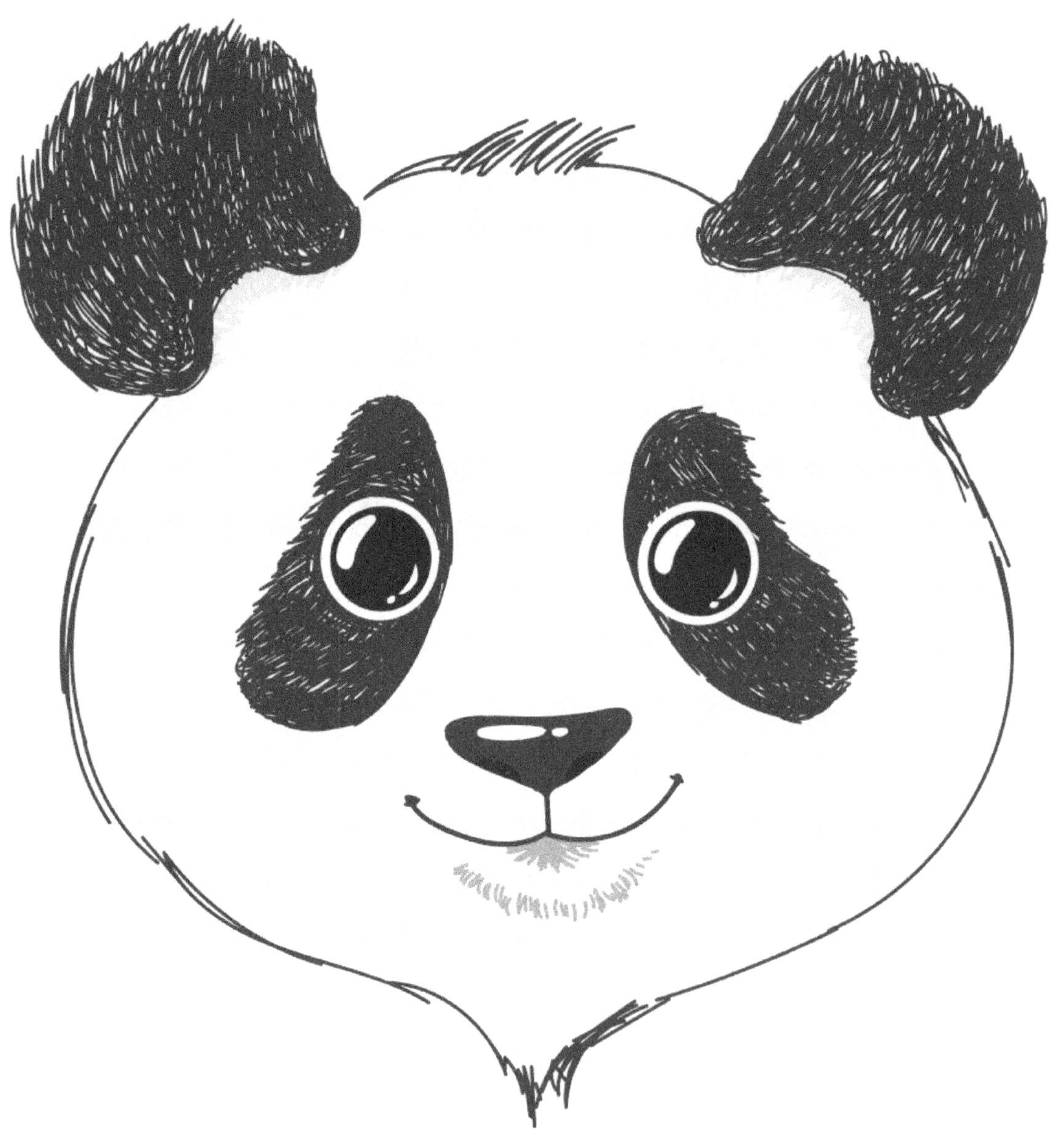